Theory Paper Grade 6 1999 A

Duration 3 hours

Candidates should answer all FIVE questions.
Write your answers on this paper — no others will be accepted.
Answers must be written clearly and neatly — otherwise marks may be lost.

TOTAL MARKS 100

15

1 Answer **ONE** section only, (a) or (b).

EITHER

(a) Indicate **ONE** chord at each of the places marked * to accompany the following melody. You may do so by writing roman numerals or any other recognised method of notation between the staves, **OR** by writing notes on the staves which provide a proper harmonic structure; but use only **ONE** of these methods.

O'Carolan, *Captain Sudley*

OR

(b) Complete the bass line and add suitable figures as necessary, *from bar 2*, at the places marked * in this passage. If you wish to use a $^5_3$ chord, leave the space under the asterisk blank, but $^5_3$ chords *must* be shown as part of a $^6_4\,^5_3$ progression or when chromatic alteration is required.

Handel, Flute Sonata No. 5 in F (adapted)

2 Writing for four-part voices (SATB) or keyboard, realise this figured bass. Assume that all chords are $^5_3$ unless otherwise shown.

15

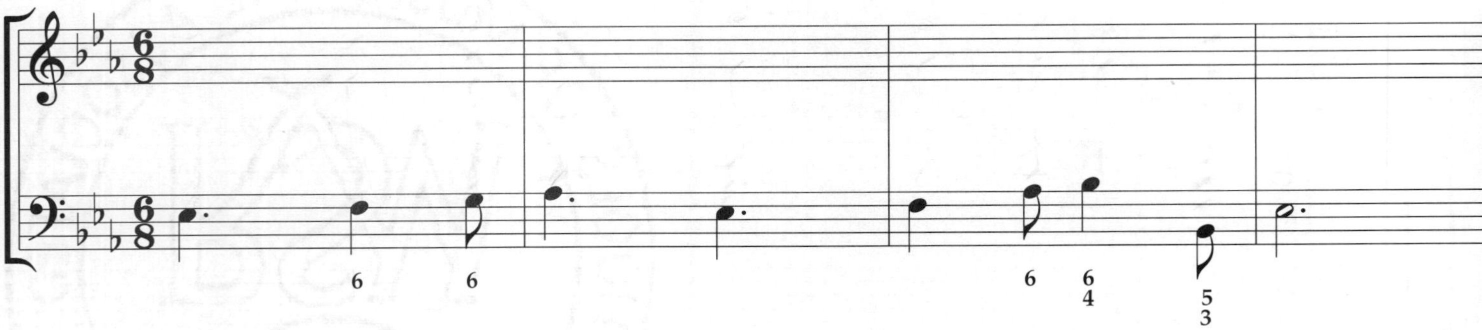

3 EITHER 20

(a) Continue this opening to form a melody for unaccompanied cello. It should end with a modulation to the subdominant and should be between eight and ten bars long. Add performance directions as appropriate and write the complete melody on the staves below.

OR

(b) Continue this opening for unaccompanied oboe to make a complete piece of not less than eight bars in length. You may make any modulation or modulations that you wish, or none if you prefer. Add performance directions as appropriate and write the complete melody on the staves below.

4 Study the extract from the second movement of Beethoven's Piano Sonata Op. 10 No. 1 on page 7, and then answer the following questions. 25

(a) In the first eight bars, draw a circle around:

(i) a dominant 7th chord in first inversion

(ii) a $^{6}_{4}\,^{5}_{3}$ (Ic–V) progression (6)

(b) Write out the right-hand part of bar 26 as you think it should be played.

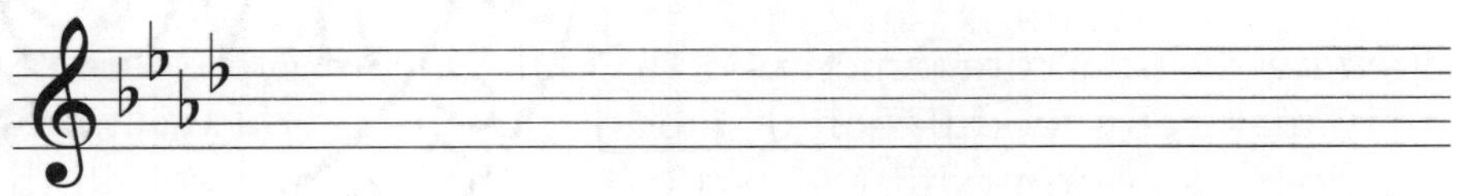

(3)

(c) Mark clearly on the score, using the appropriate capital letter for identification, one example of each of the following:

A a chromatic unaccented passing note in the right-hand part
B a chromatic accented passing note in the left-hand part
C an acciaccatura (6)

(d) Compare bars 1–4 with bars 9–12, then name a similarity and a difference:

(i) in the *melodic line* of bars 9–12

Similarity ....

Difference ....

(ii) in the *accompaniment* of bars 9–12

Similarity ....

Difference .... (4)

(e) Complete the following statements:

(i) Bars 17–18 are in the key of ....

(ii) Bars 19–20 are in the key of ....

(iii) The name given to the technical device used in bars 17–20 is a .... (6)

Adagio molto
cresc.
[cresc.]
etc.

5 Study the orchestral extract printed on pages 9 and 10, from near the start of Gounod's opera *Faust*, and then answer the questions below. 25

(a) Complete the following statements:

(i) 'a 2' in bar 31 means that ....

(ii) Two standard members of orchestral brass *not* playing here are ....

and ....

(iii) Two standard members of orchestral percussion *not* playing here are ....

and ....

(iv) The only string section which bows throughout is .... (8)

(b) Write TRUE or UNTRUE after each of these statements:

(i) The strings play an accompanying role throughout. ....

(ii) The ornament in bar 13 (oboe) is a lower mordent. .... (4)

(c) On the blank staves at the bottom of page 10, write out the parts of bars 26–28 for:

(i) clarinets as they would sound at concert pitch, and

(ii) bassoons in the bass clef underneath the clarinet parts. (5)

(d) Mark clearly on the score, using the appropriate capital letter for identification, one example of each of the following:

A a double-stopped interval of a minor 7th in a string part.

B the interval of a compound perfect 5th sounding between cello and viola.

C the interval of a compound major 3rd sounding between a pair of the same woodwind instrument.

D overlapping melodic imitation (mark ⌈ D ⌉ over the bars). (8)

Turn the page

20
25
30
2 Fl.
2 Ob.
2 Clts. in A
2 Fag.
I Vln. II
Viola
Cello
I
pp
a 2
etc.

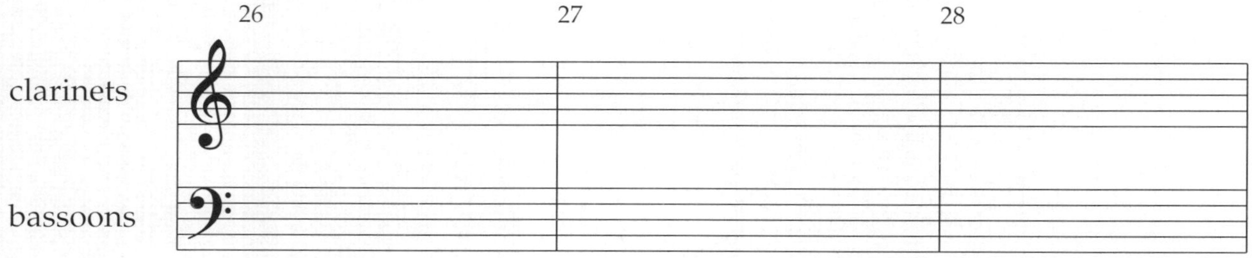
26
27
28
clarinets
bassoons

Theory Paper Grade 6 1999 B

Duration 3 hours

Candidates should answer all FIVE questions.
Write your answers on this paper — no others will be accepted.
Answers must be written clearly and neatly — otherwise marks may be lost.

TOTAL MARKS 100

1 Answer **ONE** section only, (a) or (b). 15

EITHER

(a) Indicate **ONE** chord at each of the places marked * to accompany the following melody. You may do so by writing roman numerals or any other recognised method of notation between the staves, **OR** by writing notes on the staves which provide a proper harmonic structure; but use only **ONE** of these methods.

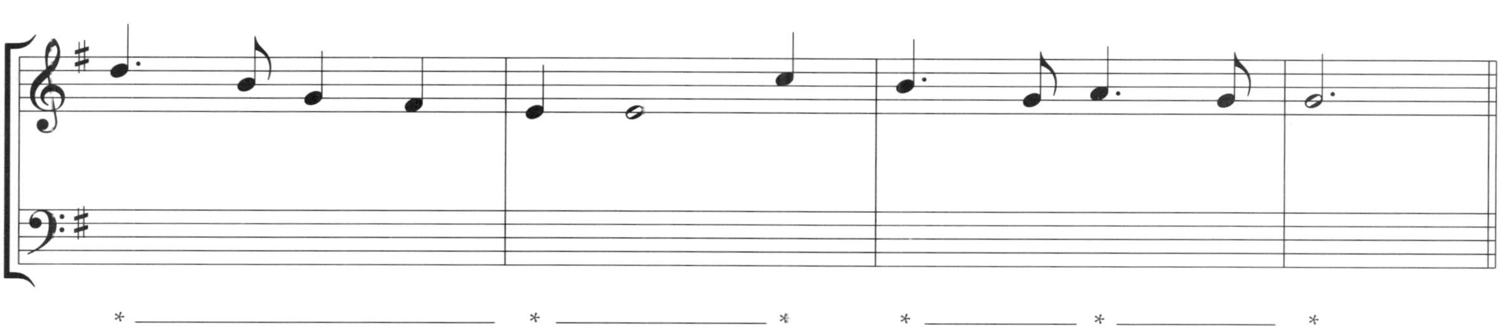

OR

(b) Complete the bass line and add suitable figures as necessary, *from the last beat of bar 2*, at the places marked * in this passage from a chorus by Purcell from his opera *Dido and Aeneas*. If you wish to use a $^{5}_{3}$ chord, leave the space under the asterisk blank, but $^{5}_{3}$ chords *must* be shown as part of a $^{6}_{4}\,^{5}_{3}$ progression or when chromatic alteration is required.

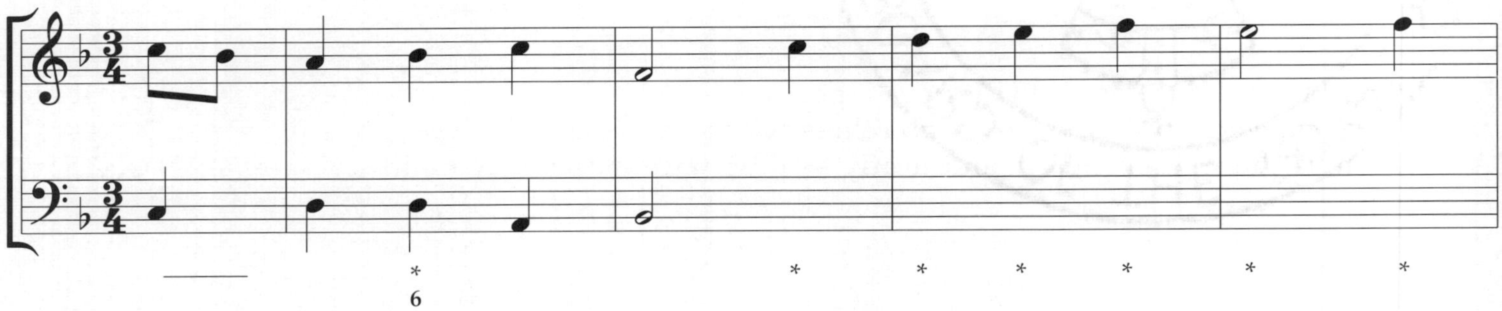

2 Writing for four-part voices (SATB) or keyboard, realise this figured bass. Assume that all chords are $^{5}_{3}$ unless otherwise shown.

15

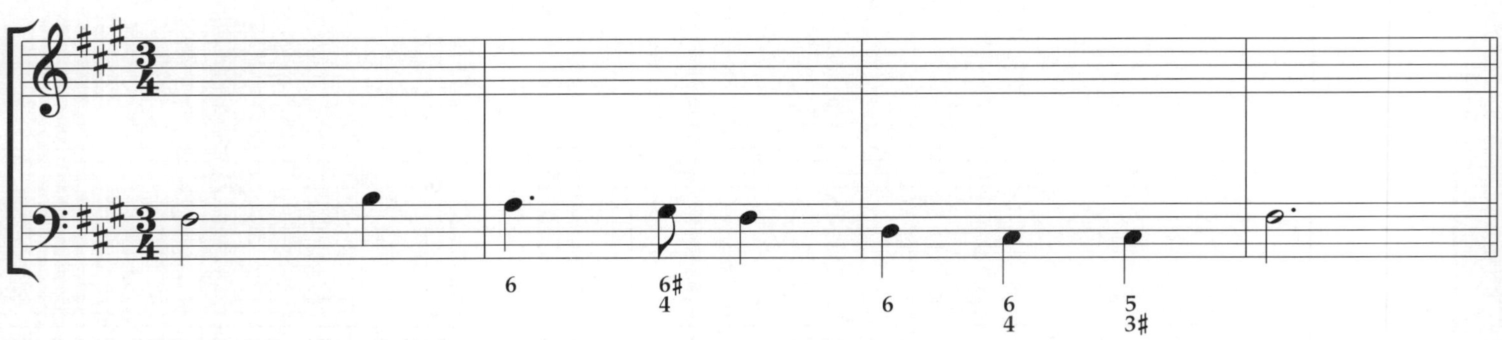

3 EITHER

20

(a) Continue this opening to form a melody for unaccompanied violin. It should end with a modulation to the dominant and should be between eight and ten bars long. Add performance directions as appropriate and write the complete melody on the staves below.

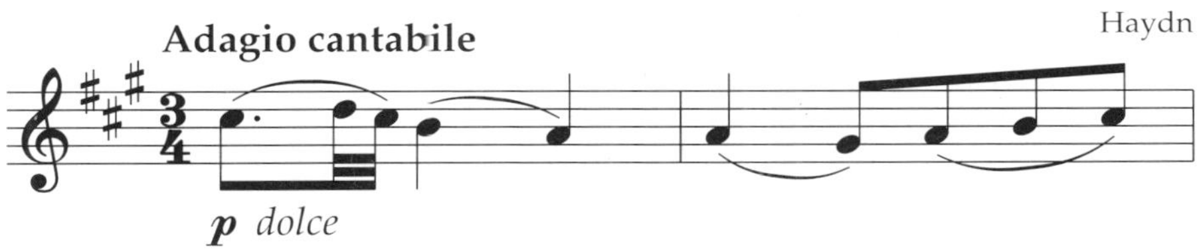

OR

(b) Continue this opening for unaccompanied bassoon to make a complete piece of not less than eight bars in length. You may make any modulation or modulations that you wish, or none if you prefer. Add performance directions as appropriate and write the complete melody on the staves below.

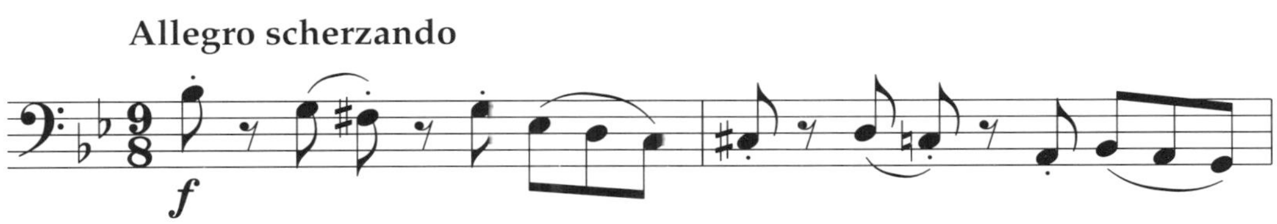

4 Study the extract on page 15 from Grieg's *Holberg Suite* for piano, and then answer the following questions. 25

(a) Mark clearly on the score, using the appropriate capital letter for identification, one example of each of the following:

A a melodic note of anticipation in the first eight bars

B a bar showing melodic imitation between the hands

C an acciaccatura (6)

(b) Write out the top line of the right-hand part of bar 4 as you think it should be played.

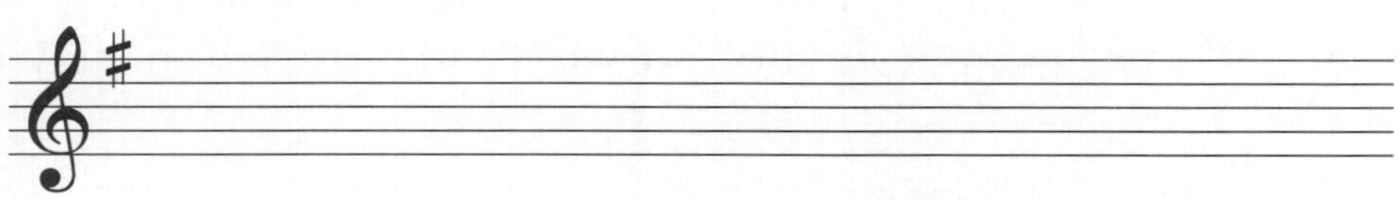

(3)

(c) Name the chords marked * in bars 2 and 9, stating the position of each chord and whether it is major, minor, augmented or diminished.

Bar 2 .... Key ....

Bar 9 .... Key .... (8)

(d) (i) Show the phrase structure of the right-hand melody of bars 17–22 by drawing ⌐‾‾‾‾‾‾‾‾‾‾‾¬ over the phrases. (4)

(ii) Trace the modulations in bars 17–24, naming the keys and giving the appropriate bar numbers.

....

....

....

.... (4)

Andante espressivo ♩ = 52
cantabile
p legato
poco più mosso
p
mf
p
pp
cresc.
poco a poco meno mosso
p
cresc.
molto
etc.

5 Study the extract printed on pages 17 and 18, from the end of a trio from the opera *L'Elisir d'Amore* ('The Elixir of Love') by Donizetti, and then answer the questions below. The orchestral part is reduced for piano. | 25 |

(a) (i) Name the key at the start. ....

(ii) In this key, name the chords marked * in bars 5 and 7 of the piano part. State the position of each chord and whether it is major, minor, augmented or diminished.

bar 5 ....

bar 7 .... (7)

(b) Mark clearly on the score, using the appropriate capital letter for identification, one example of each of the following:

A a chromatic lower auxiliary note in the right hand of the piano part, over a submediant chord.

B a place where the baritone soloist imitates the melody of the first bar of the soprano solo part.

C a place where the tenor soloist imitates the melody of the first bar of the soprano solo part.

D a false (cross) relation in the notes of the piano part.

E a $\begin{smallmatrix}6\\4\end{smallmatrix}\ \begin{smallmatrix}5\\3\end{smallmatrix}\ \begin{smallmatrix}5\\3\end{smallmatrix}$ (Ic–V–I) cadential progression in the piano part, in the tonic key.

F syncopation in the vocal parts. (12)

(c) Complete the following statements:

(i) The vocal parts in bars 9–12 could be described as homophonic, which means ....

.... (2)

(ii) This trio uses solo soprano, tenor and baritone voices. Two other voice categories not used here are the female voice .... , and the male voice .... (4)

Turn the page

10
fa, sì che mi fa, sì che mi
drà, se n'av - - ve - - drà, se n'av - - ve - -
qua, se non va via, sì via di
15
fa, che mi fa, che mi fa, che mi fa, che mi fa.
drà, sì do - man, sì do - man, s'av - ve - drà, s'av - ve - drà,
qua, se non va via, va via di qua.

Theory Paper Grade 6 1999 C

Duration 3 hours

Candidates should answer all FOUR questions.
Write your answers on this paper — no others will be accepted.
Answers must be written clearly and neatly — otherwise marks may be lost.

TOTAL MARKS 100

1 Answer ONE section only, (a) or (b). 15

EITHER

(a) Indicate ONE chord at each of the places marked * to accompany the following melody. You may do so by writing roman numerals or any other recognised method of notation between the staves, OR by writing notes on the staves which provide a proper harmonic structure; but use only ONE of these methods.

Gibbons, *Song 46*

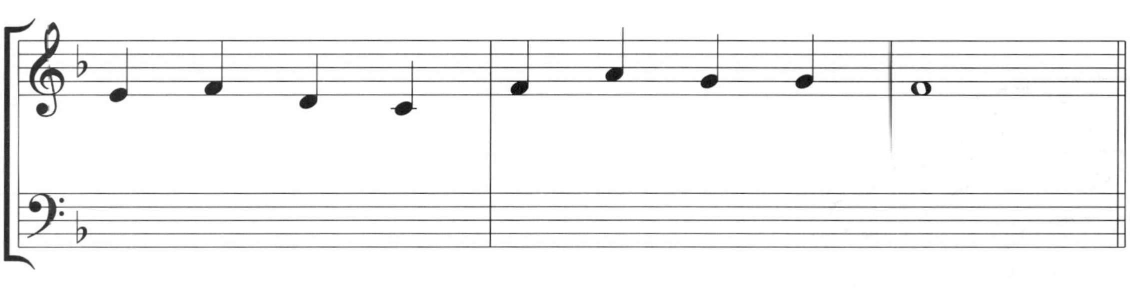

OR

(b) Complete the bass line and add suitable figures as necessary, *from bar 2*, at the places marked * in this passage. If you wish to use a $^{5}_{3}$ chord, leave the space under the asterisk blank, but $^{5}_{3}$ chords *must* be shown as part of a $^{6}_{4}\,^{5}_{3}$ progression or when chromatic alteration is required.

Corelli, Concerto Grosso No. 8

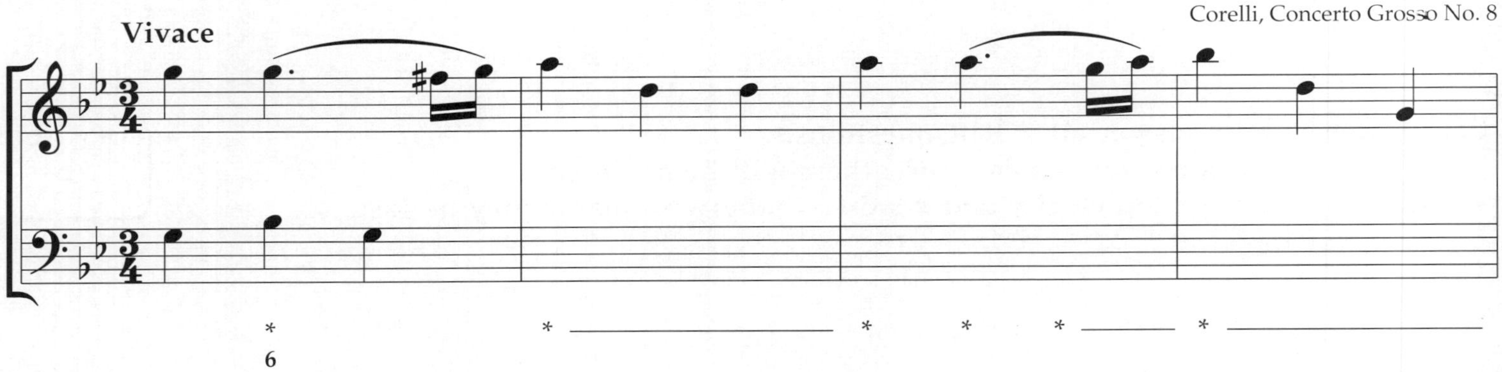

2 Writing for four-part voices (SATB) or keyboard, realise this figured bass. Assume that all chords are $^{5}_{3}$ unless otherwise shown. 15

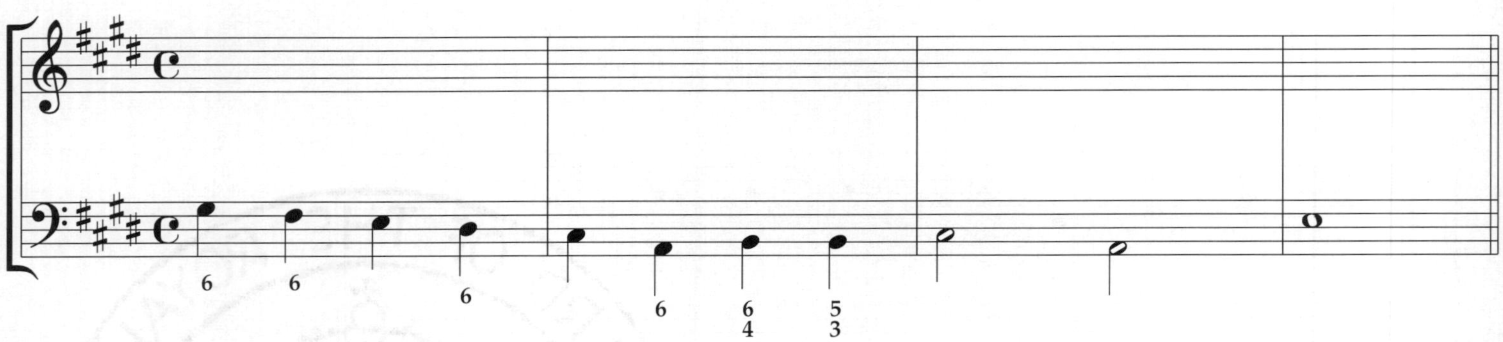

3 EITHER

20

(a) Continue this opening to form a melody for unaccompanied flute. It should end with a modulation to the relative major and should be between eight and ten bars long. Add performance directions as appropriate and write the complete melody on the staves below.

OR

(b) Continue this opening for unaccompanied trombone to make a complete piece of not less than eight bars in length. You may make any modulation or modulations that you wish, or none if you prefer. Add performance directions as appropriate and write the complete melody on the staves below.

Intermezzo
Allegretto con moto
Violin 1
Violin 2
Viola
Cello
pizz.
arco
tr

4 Study the extract on page 22 from Mendelssohn's String Quartet Op. 13, and then answer the following questions. 50

(a) Mark clearly on the score, using the appropriate capital letter for identification, one example of each of the following:

A a written-out upward appoggiatura in the first eight bars.

B a triple-stop which is a dominant 7th of C major in the first eight bars.

C a plucked note, marked to be played on an open string, in the second section.

D the progression $\substack{6\\4}\ \substack{7\\5\\\sharp}\ \substack{5\\3}$ (Ic–V^7–I) in the tonic key.

E a perfect cadence in C major in the second section. (10)

(b) Name the chords marked * in bars 3, 9 and 22. State the position of each chord and whether it is major, minor, augmented or diminished.

Bar 3 .... Key ....

Bar 9 .... Key ....

Bar 22 .... Key .... (12)

(c) The violin 1 motif in bar 1 is used in E minor in the second section. Name the instruments concerned, giving bar numbers.

....

.... (8)

(d) Write out the viola part of bar 12 as you think it should be played.

(3)

(e) Music for string quartet is sometimes arranged for wind instruments. Write out the part for violin 1 in bars 15–17 as it would appear for a clarinet in B♭ to sound at the same pitch. Use the necessary key signature.

clarinet in B♭ (4)

(f) Compare bars 5–6 with bars 23–24, then point out similarities or differences in each of the following:

(i) the violin 1 melody ....

(ii) the harmony ....

(iii) the rhythm and part-writing for violin 2, viola and cello ....

....

.... (5)

(g) Name the intervals formed between the bottom and top notes of the viola part in bar 5.

first beat ....

second beat .... (4)

(h) Write TRUE or UNTRUE after each of the following statements.

(i) Only two instruments of the four have double stops. ....

(ii) The phrase structure is in regular, four-bar phrases throughout. .... (4)

Theory Paper Grade 6 1999 S

Duration 3 hours

Candidates should answer all FIVE questions.
Write your answers on this paper — no others will be accepted.
Answers must be written clearly and neatly — otherwise marks may be lost.

TOTAL MARKS 100

1 Answer **ONE** section only, (a) or (b). 15

EITHER

(a) Indicate **ONE** chord at each of the places marked * to accompany the following melody. You may do so by writing roman numerals or any other recognised method of notation between the staves, **OR** by writing notes on the staves which provide a proper harmonic structure; but use only **ONE** of these methods.

OR

(b) Complete the bass line and add suitable figures as necessary, *from bar 3*, at the places marked * in this passage adapted from an air by John Gay from *The Beggar's Opera*. If you wish to use a $^{5}_{3}$ chord, leave the space under the asterisk blank, but $^{5}_{3}$ chords *must* be shown as part of a $^{6}_{4}\,^{5}_{3}$ progression or when chromatic alteration is required.

2 Writing for four-part voices (SATB) or keyboard, realise this figured bass. Assume that all chords are $^{5}_{3}$ unless otherwise shown.

15

3 EITHER 20

(a) Continue this opening to form a melody for unaccompanied clarinet. It should end with a modulation to the dominant and should be between eight and ten bars long. Add performance directions as appropriate and write the complete melody on the staves below.

OR

(b) Continue this opening for unaccompanied violin to make a complete piece of not less than eight bars in length. You may make any modulation or modulations that you wish, or none if you prefer. Add performance directions as appropriate and write the complete melody on the staves below.

4 Study the extract printed on page 29 from Haydn's Mass in B♭ (*Harmonienmesse*) with the orchestral part reduced for piano, and then answer the following questions. 25

(a) Mark clearly on the score, using the appropriate capital letter for identification, one example of each of the following:

(i) in the introduction (bars 1–12):

A a dominant 7th chord in third inversion (V^7d)

B a chord of the subdominant in first inversion (IVb)

C the first of three successive progressions of $\begin{smallmatrix}6\\4\end{smallmatrix}\ \begin{smallmatrix}5\\3\end{smallmatrix}$ (IVc–I) on the tonic note;

(ii) and in the vocal part:

D a bar containing two accented passing notes in the dominant key. (8)

(b) Write out the melodic line of bar 11 as you think it should be performed.

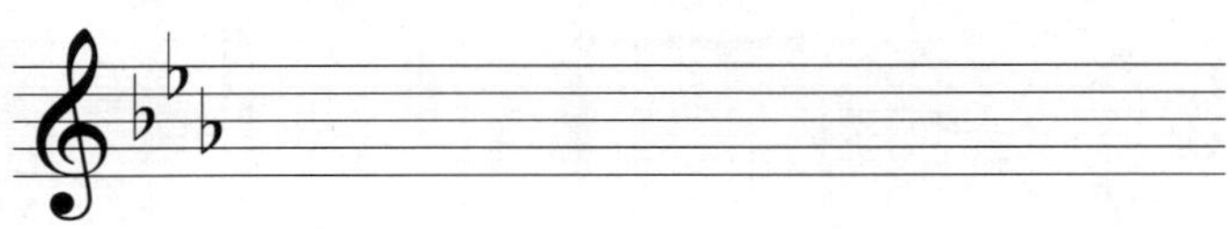

(3)

(c) In the orchestral original the melodic line of bars 1–4 is played by a clarinet in B♭. Write out the part as it would appear for the player, using the necessary key signature.

(4)

(d) Draw a circle round each of the notes of the vocal line in bar 30 which are not essential to the harmony. What is the name given to these notes of melodic decoration? (3)

.... (2)

(e) (i) Name two similarities and two differences between bars 13–16 and bars 25–28.

Similarities 1. ....

2. ....

Differences 1. ....

2. .... (4)

(ii) Where has this melodic and harmonic material appeared earlier? Bars .... (1)

Allegretto
espr.
Solo Alto
Gra - - ti-as a - - gi-mus,
a - gi-mus ti-bi pro - pter mag - nam glo - - ri - am tu - am
rit.
espr.
pro - pter mag - nam, pro - pter mag - nam glo - - ri - am tu - - - am.
espr.
a tempo
etc.

5 Study the extract printed on page 31, from the third movement of the *Fantastic Symphony* by Berlioz, and then answer the questions below.

25

(a) Which instrument(s):

(i) are marked to pluck the strings throughout? ....

(ii) only bow the strings? ....

(iii) are written an octave apart throughout the whole extract? .... and ....

(iv) plays the melodic interval of a diminished 5th? .... (8)

(b) (i) Write out the clarinet part of bars 7–8 as it would sound at concert pitch, using the appropriate key signature.

(4)

(ii) Of which part is this an 'echo'? Instrument .... bars .... (2)

(iii) Which note is different in the 'echo'? Note .... in bar .... (1)

(iv) What else is different between the original notes and the 'echo' in performance? .... (2)

(c) Complete the following statements:

(i) Bar .... is a one-bar sequence of the melody and harmony of bar ....

(ii) The flute and .... fill in the breaks in the clarinet solo and their parts are mainly based on the intervals of a ....

(iii) There is a chromatic, lower auxiliary note in the viola part in bar .... and the written note is ....

(iv) The number I° at the beginning of the clarinet part means .... (8)

Adagio
2 Clarinetti in B♭
I° dolce
Violino 1
Violino 2
sempre pizz.
Viola
sempre pizz.
Violoncello e Contrabasso
pizz.
Solo
2 Fl.
Cl. B♭
Echo
Vl.
Vla.
Vc. Cb.
ancora più
ancora più
poco
cresc.
etc.
cresc. un poco
cresc. un poco
arco
Vc.
div.
pizz.
pizz.
Cb.

ABRSM PUBLISHING

The Associated Board of the Royal Schools of Music (Publishing) Limited

14 Bedford Square
London WC1B 3JG
United Kingdom

www.abrsmpublishing.co.uk

ISBN 1-86096-080-4

9 781860 960802